Printed in the United States of America

First Printing, 2019

ISBN: **978-1-950464-00-5**

www.OffBeatReads.com

This book is dedicated to:

Boys; who should be as manly as they want to be.

And to:

Girls; who are smart and strong enough without politicians telling them that

they need a village to make it.

The Politically
Incorrect
Alphabet Book

Assimilate

If you wish to live in the United States, you should be willing to accept and live by the values of The Constitution. One does not enter another country to hate or alter the fundamental beliefs of that country.

Boy

A male child.

See: M

Christmas

This is a holiday many Americans celebrate. The reason why does not matter. If someone does not like the holiday, they simply should not celebrate it.

Dumb

Some people, called progressives, are incapable of rational thinking. They like to be angry, yell without knowledge, get overly emotional, and hate those who think differently than them. They are dumb.

Emotions

Emotions are sometimes the result of things that happen around us. Emotions should rarely drive our decisions. Some people get overly emotional for attention, some even burst into uncontrollable tantrums due to immaturity.

Female

Humans with cells that lack Y chromosomes (XO or XX).
This fact cannot be altered by delusion.

Girl

A female child.
See: F

Homosexual

Someone that is attracted to those of the same gender.
Incidentally, using reasoning, gender must exist in order for
homosexuality to be possible. People have a fundamental
right to live the way they choose or in accordance with
the way they are born. In the U.S. we don't hurt others because
they are different, nor do we try to force others
into our way of thinking.

I

"I" means you alone are valuable. Being part of a collective is not necessary. Making the most of the life you've been given while being loving and charitable is the moral high ground—while sacrificing self for attention or "Feeling good" is real selfishness.

Job

A job is work that someone does in exchange for compensation (usually money). By nature, a large percentage of progressive-minded people don't have jobs. They believe things should be given to them because they can't make it in life without robbing from those who have.

Karma

The belief that people's actions, good or bad, have a way of coming back to them.

Used in a sentence:
"Hillary Clinton losing the election was sweet karma."

Liar

Someone who doesn't tell the truth.

Practice: Use *liar* in a sentence with the name *Hillary Clinton*.

Male

Humans that have cells that contain a Y chromosome (XY).
This fact cannot be altered by delusion.

Nazi

Someone that belongs to the National Socialist German Workers' Party. Socialists of today try to make others believe President Donald Trump is a Nazi, when in fact he is not. Donald Trump does not believe in a totalitarian government. Socialists do.
Ironic, huh?

Offensive

Something that is considered hurtful, negative, hateful.
People that consider many things offensive should be minding
their own business.

Pee

If you are a male, go to the male bathroom to pee.
If you are a female, go to the female bathroom to pee.
If you want to go pee in the other bathroom,
you must either change your sex or
seek help with a professional.

Quit

To stop something, usually prematurely.

"Bernie Sanders went to college, but at some point he obviously quit learning."

Rob

To take something from someone else.

Used in a run-on sentence:
"Because socialist politicians want to gain power they want you envious when others have more than you this way you vote for them because you think they will make things more equal by punishing success when in fact they will never be able to objectively make anything fair but they have the emotionally driven hating corporations and thinking it is right to literally rob from some and give to others and somehow that is fair but it never works it causes economies and civilized societies to fail and crash hard ideally people should live in society where they are totally free AND responsible for their own lives not told what to do by power-seeking politicians."

Slum

What happens to any city in which a progressive holds a public office.

Trigger

This is part of a gun, typically pulled by your index finger when you want to shoot a home intruder, a target, or are hunting. This word is also used to refer to words or actions that cause immature people to become angry or sad.

United States

The first and only country to take individual liberty to it's maximum by making it a constitutional guarantee. Other countries try to copy certain aspects, but fall short. The government gives too much control to the so-called leaders and to the State (with a capital S). Despite the greatness of our nation, radicals water down our freedom and seek to take rights away by convincing people they are victims or that things are unfair.

Vixen

A smokin' hot woman.
(aka: a woman in the MAGA Movement;
it's a sapiosexual thing.)

Wealth

A Wealthy person isn't bad, just like a poor person isn't bad.
Having more money just means you have more of the common tool
of trade: money. If you think money is evil, raise chickens or sew
quilts to barter with.

Xenophobia

Hating or fearing others for their culture or race.

Example: In recent years, those who want strong borders have been accused of xenophobia. In reality, these patriotic people usually have guns, thus fear little. They simply want people to enter the U.S legally, and for immigrant crime (which is underreported) to cease.

Yellow

John Wayne would say, "What are ya, yella?"

Zygote

It's the living cell you became when your dad's sperm fertilized your mom's ovary.

The End

www.ingramcontent.com/pod-product-compliance
Lightning Source LLC
Chambersburg PA
CBHW060836270326
41933CB00002B/100